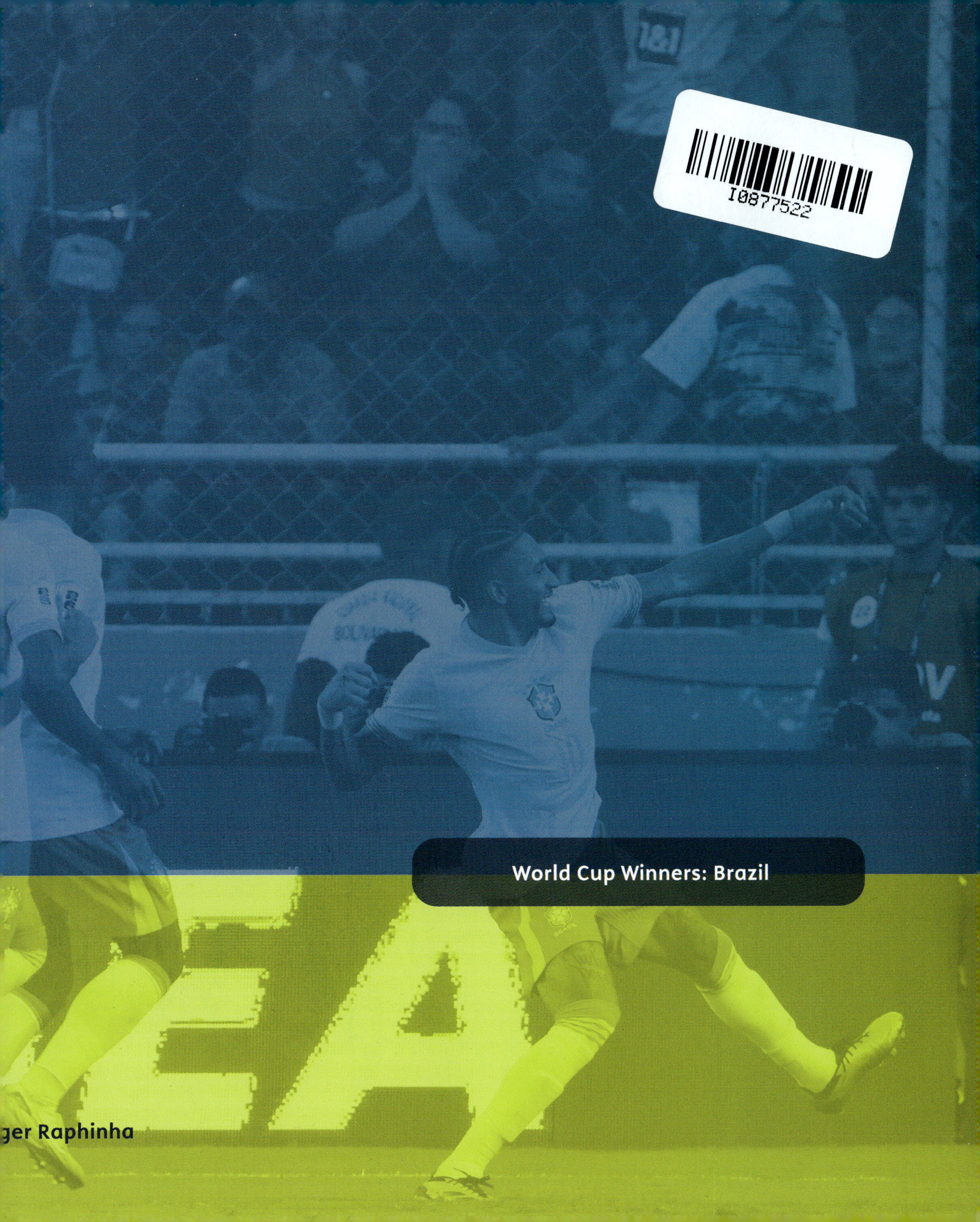

World Cup Winners: Brazil

ger Raphinha

Striker Romário

WORLD CUP WINNERS

BRAZIL

JAMES BARRY

CREATIVE EDUCATION / CREATIVE PAPERBACKS

Published by Creative Education and Creative Paperbacks
P.O. Box 227, Mankato, Minnesota 56002
Creative Education and Creative Paperbacks
are imprints of The Creative Company
www.thecreativecompany.us

Book design by Blue Design (www.bluedes.com)

Images by Getty Images/Alessandro Sabattini, 2, 3, 5, 10, 16, 19, Edilzon Gamez, 1, Eric Verhoeven/Soccrates Images, 20, Hector Vivas - FIFA, 6, Heidtmann/picture alliance, 15, Jam Media, cover, 7; Unsplash/Agustin Diaz Gargiulo, 9; Wikimedia Commons/Brazilian National Archives, 12, public domain, 4, 24
Every effort has been made to contact copyright holders for material reproduced in this book. Any omissions will be rectified in subsequent printings if notice is given to the publisher.

Library of Congress Cataloging-in-Publication Data
Names: Barry, James (Author of children's books) author.
Title: Brazil / James Barry.
Description: Mankato, Minnesota : Creative Education and Creative Paperbacks, 2026. | Series: Creative sports. World Cup winners | Includes index. | Audience: Ages 7–10 | Audience: Grades 2–3 | Summary: "No nation has won more FIFA World Cups than Brazil-five in all! This elementary title follows Pelé, Romário, Zico, Neymar, and more through nail-biting matches as the Canary Squad "sambas" its way to soccer fame"– Provided by publisher.
Identifiers: LCCN 2024046124 (print) | LCCN 2024046125 (ebook) | ISBN 9798889895992 (library binding) | ISBN 9781682777657 (paperback) | ISBN 9798889896791 (ebook)
Subjects: LCSH: Soccer–Brazil–History–Juvenile literature. | World Cup (Soccer)–History–Juvenile literature.
Classification: LCC GV944.B7 B38 2026 (print) | LCC GV944.B7 (ebook) | DDC 796.3340981–dc23/eng/202412/12
LC record available at https://lccn.loc.gov/2024046124
LC ebook record available at https://lccn.loc.gov/2024046125

Printed in India

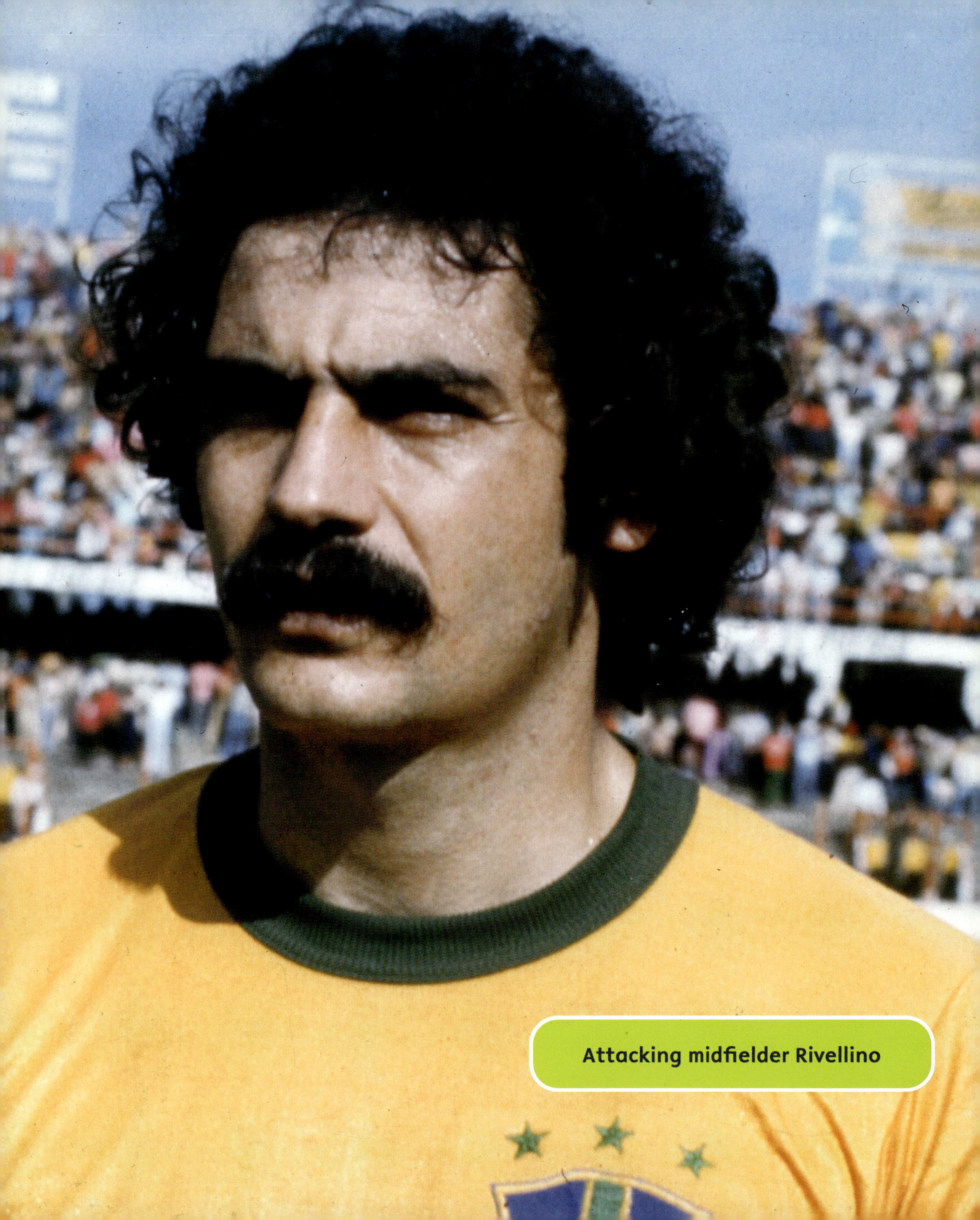

Attacking midfielder Rivellino

Left-winger Neymar

CONTENTS

Home of the Team

Brazil is the biggest country in South America. It takes up half the continent. It contains most of the Amazon rainforest. Scientists say it's made up of more than 390 billion trees.

Brazilians skip work to cheer on the national soccer team, and for good reason. It's won more World Cups than any other team. The World Cup is a worldwide soccer tournament. Countries make teams of their best players. Every four years, they compete to become world champion.

Attacking midfielder Ronaldinho

Team Traditions

The Brazil national team is nicknamed the "Canary Squad" for its bright yellow jersey. It's known for playing "samba" soccer. This is a creative style named for Brazil's national dance—the samba. Brazil's greatest **rival** is Argentina. The two nations have one of the biggest soccer rivalries in the world. When they play, it's called the "Battle of the Americas."

Brazil at the 1950 World Cup

Team History

Brazil played its first match in 1914. In 1930, Brazil played in the first World Cup. The team lost in the first stage of play. It wasn't until the 1950s that Brazil became a world soccer power. The nation hosted the 1950 World Cup. The team made it to the championship game against Uruguay. But it lost in front of about 200,000 spectators. It was a national tragedy. It's still one of the biggest upsets in soccer history.

In 1958, Brazil won its first World Cup. The team defeated the host country Sweden 5–2 in the championship game. Led by young star Pelé, the Brazil national team entered its first golden era. It won the next World Cup in 1962 and another in 1970. It became the first nation to win three World Cups. The 1970 Brazil team won all six of its games. It is one of the greatest teams of all time.

Defender Carlos Alberto Torres wins the World Cup for Brazil in 1970.

Striker Ronaldo

After winning in 1970, Brazil lost in the next five World Cups. In the 1990s, it came back to its winning ways. In 1994, Brazil won another World Cup. It beat Italy in the final match. In 2002, Brazil won its fifth World Cup. The team was led by the "Three R's," Ronaldo, Rivaldo, and Ronaldinho, three of its best players. The second golden era was complete.

Team Stars

Brazil has had too many soccer stars to name. Pelé was a member of the country's first three World Cup-winning teams. He was known as "The King." Many players and fans think he was the greatest player of all time. Right-winger Garrincha helped Brazil to its first two World Cups. Brazil never lost a match when Pelé and Garrincha started together. **Playmaker** Sócrates was known for his great passes. Zico scored 48 goals in 71 **caps** for Brazil.

Forward Pelé

Left-winger Neymar

Romário won the 1994 World Cup **Golden Ball**. He was one of the best goal scorers ever. **Striker** Ronaldo led Brazil to three straight World Cup finals. Ronaldinho was known as "The Wizard" for his magical skills. In 2023, Neymar became Brazil's all-time leader in goals. Fans hope he can lead Brazil to its sixth World Cup soon.

About the Brazil National Team

First year: 1914

Team colors: yellow, green, dark blue, light blue, white

Home stadium: Maracanã Stadium

WORLD CUP VICTORIES:

1958, 5–2 over Sweden

1962, 3–1 over Czechoslovakia

1970, 4–1 over Italy

1994, 0–0, defeated Italy 3–2 in penalties

2002, 2–0 over Germany https://www.cbf.com.br/

WEBSITE

https://www.cbf.com.br/

Glossary

cap—an official match played for a national soccer team

Golden Ball—an award given to the best player at each World Cup

playmaker—a player who controls the flow of the team's play and makes passes leading to goals

rival—a team that plays extra hard against another team

striker—a player who mainly attacks and scores goals, rather than defends

Forward Pelé in 1958

Index